W9-BWF-412

974.5
WIN

BOOK CHARGING CARD

3488000823125

Accession No. _____ Call No. 974.5 WIN

Author Winans, Jay D.

Title Rhode Island

Date Loaned	Borrower's Name	Date Returned

974.5
WIN
Winans, Jay D.
Rhode Island

RHODE ISLAND

Jay D. Winans

Published by Weigl Publishers Inc.
123 South Broad Street, Box 227
Mankato, MN   56002
USA
Web site: http://www.weigl.com

Library of Congress Cataloging-in-Publication Data available upon request from the publisher. Fax: (507) 388-2746 for the attention of the Publishing Records Department.

ISBN 1-930954-84-0

Printed in the United States of America
1 2 3 4 5 6 7 8 9 10   05 04 03 02 01

Editor
Jennifer Nault
Copy Editor
Jared Keen
Designers
Warren Clark
Terry Paulhus
Layout
Katherine Phillips
Photo Researchers
Rachel Doe
Tina Schwartzenberger

Photograph Credits

Cover: Maple leaves (Corel Corporation), Schooner (Rhode Island Tourism); **Kindra Clineff Photography:** pages 3T, 3M, 4T, 4BR, 5T, 6T, 6B, 7T, 7B, 8T, 8B, 9B, 11T, 11BL, 12T, 13B, 18B, 19B, 20T, 20BL, 20BR, 21B, 22, 26T, 26B, 29R; **Corel Corporation:** pages 10BR, 11BR, 15B; **EyeWire Corporation:** page 25T; **Samuel Hough-Owl at the Bridge:** page 15T; **International Tennis Hall of Fame:** page 27B; **Martha Jones:** page 23T; **National Archives of Canada:** page 17T (C2061); **PhotoDisc Inc:** pages 3B, 25B; **Photofest:** page 28; **Rhode Island Historical Society:** pages 17B, 18T; **Rhode Island Tourism:** pages 4BL, 7BL, 9T, 10T, 10BL, 12B, 13T, 14T, 14B, 19T, 21T, 23BL, 23BR, 24T, 24B, 27T; **University of Rhode Island:** page 29L; **Marilyn "Angel" Wynn:** pages 16T, 16B.

CONTENTS

Introduction 4

Land and Climate 8

Natural Resources 9

Plants and Animals 10

Tourism 12

Industry 13

Goods and Services 14

First Nations 16

Explorers and Missionaries 17

Early Settlers 18

Population 20

Politics and Government 21

Cultural Groups 22

Arts and Entertainment 24

Sports 26

Brain Teasers 28

For More Information 30

Glossary 31

Index 32

Much of Rhode Island's coastline is rocky, but the state also has over 100 miles of beautiful sandy beaches.

QUICK FACTS

The official name of the state is The State of Rhode Island and Providence Plantations.

Providence is the capital of Rhode Island.

Rhode Island entered the Union on May 29, 1790, as the last of the original thirteen states.

The state flag has a ship's anchor and a circle of thirteen stars representing the original thirteen states. The state motto, "Hope," is displayed on a blue ribbon beneath the anchor.

INTRODUCTION

You may need to squint to see Rhode Island on a map, but it is not difficult to see that this state is brimming with industry, history, and culture. Rhode Island is the smallest state in the United States, covering only 1,213 square miles. In fact, Rhode Island could fit into the state of Texas 220 times! Despite its small size, Rhode Island is an important industrial state.

Rhode Island is one of the New England states, along with Maine, New Hampshire, Vermont, Massachusetts, and Connecticut. It is graced by a beautiful shoreline along the Atlantic Ocean. Rhode Island has a 40-mile coastline. When you include the state's bays and islands, however, the coastline measures 384 miles. With this in mind, it should come as no surprise that the state's official nickname is "The Ocean State." The Atlantic Ocean, the second-largest ocean in the world, has greatly influenced the state's economy and its people. The coast is the most important commercial area, lending itself to a vibrant fishing industry. Since the twentieth century, the call of the coast has attracted large numbers of visitors, making tourism yet another important economic activity in the state.

The 213-year-old Jamestown Windmill on Conanicut Island was recently restored to its original condition.

Getting There

Rhode Island lies along the coast of the Atlantic Ocean, just south of Massachusetts and north of New York harbor. Rhode Island shares a border with two other states—Connecticut lies to the west, and Massachusetts forms the northern and eastern boundary. Rhode Island's southwest corner shares a water border with New York. The rest of the state borders the large coastline of Narragansett Bay and the waters of Rhode Island Sound.

Ferries provide transportation links between the mainland and the various islands in Narragansett Bay, including the popular Block Island.

Travelers can get to Rhode Island by land, sea, or air. Interstate Highways 95 and 295 are the main roadways from Connecticut and Massachusetts. Numerous train lines serve the state, giving travelers the choice of riding on Amtrak, Conrail, or the Providence and Worcester Railroad lines. Rhode Island's main airport is T. F. Green International Airport in Warwick. Conveniently located within a short drive of Boston, Cape Cod, Newport, and Providence, the T. F. Green International Airport serves many New England travelers.

QUICK FACTS

Although islands such as Newport and Block Islands are part of the state, most of Rhode Island is not an island at all!

Its long coastline makes Rhode Island easily accessible by boat or ferry. Narragansett Bay is a welcome harbor for ocean travelers. Providence and Newport are the most popular ports for oceangoers.

St. Mary's, Rhode Island's oldest Roman Catholic parish was founded in 1828. The church was the site of the wedding of Jacqueline Bouvier to John Fitzgerald Kennedy in 1953.

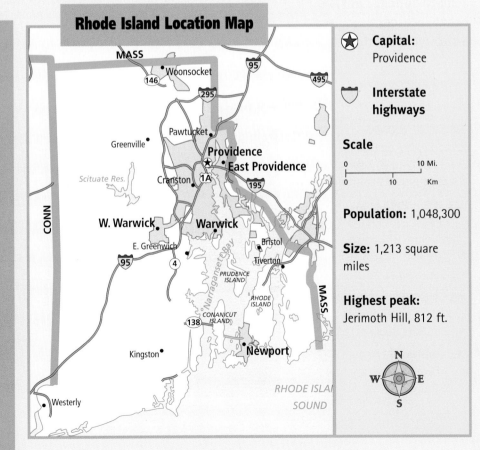

Rhode Island Location Map

Capital: Providence

Interstate highways

Scale

Population: 1,048,300

Size: 1,213 square miles

Highest peak: Jerimoth Hill, 812 ft.

Rhode Island is known for its independent nature. The state was founded in 1636 by Roger Williams after he was banished from a colony in Plymouth, Massachusetts for his religious views. Williams and others established a settlement nearby and called it Providence. They welcomed people whose religious beliefs were not **tolerated** by the other colonies.

During the American Revolution, Rhode Island was the first state to declare itself independent of England. Rhode Island's independent spirit was still strong toward the end of the American Revolution. It was the last of the original thirteen colonies to **ratify** the U.S. Constitution. Before signing, Rhode Island demanded the addition of the Bill of Rights, which guarantees individual liberties.

Rhode Island was one of the original thirteen colonies to form the United States. The nation's founding fathers, Thomas Jefferson and John Adams, recognized Roger Williams's quest for freedom and tolerance. Many of Williams's ideas are found in the First Amendment: freedom of religion, freedom of speech, and freedom of public assembly.

Rhode Island's Federal Blues, a militia founded in 1798, participate in parades and historical re-enactments.

QUICK FACTS

Providence means "the care and guidance of God or nature over the creatures of the earth."

There are more than 100 beaches in the resort communities of Newport, Narragansett, Watch Hill, and Block Island.

Many important events in early U.S. history took place in New England.

Some coniferous trees are grown on tree farms, supplying spruce, fir, and pine trees.

Little Compton has a cemetery dating back to the American Revolution.

The port of Galilee is home to a large oceangoing fishing fleet. Diesel-powered fishing trawlers catch flounder, haddock, and lobster.

Rhode Island prospered throughout the nineteenth century and attracted some of the country's wealthiest citizens. Many came to the state to take part in the commercial opportunities of Narragansett Bay.

Today, the economy enjoys modest growth based on wholesale and retail sales, real estate, tourism, and, to a lesser extent, the manufacture of silverware, jewelry, and electronic products. Agriculture and fishing remain strong and valued traditional industries in Rhode Island. Still, in the latter part of the twentieth century, declines in both fishing and agriculture prompted the government to plan programs to protect farms and orchards, coastal environments, and fish stocks.

An emerging industry in the state is closely tied to Rhode Island's coastal location. The state is making a name for itself in the field of **oceanographic** research. The oceanographic research program at the University of Rhode Island is recognized as one of the best in the nation.

QUICK FACTS

The state song is "Rhode Island, It's for Me" by Charlie Hall.

Rhode Island's greatest natural resource is Narragansett Bay. A large natural inlet that runs almost the length of the state's coastline, the bay made commercial activity easier for Rhode Islanders. It helped create great wealth in the state.

The world's largest bug is a 58-foot blue termite, located on the roof of New England Pest Control in Providence.

new england
pest control

There are many fresh produce stands found in Rhode Island.

Block Island, located 10 miles off Rhode Island's southern shore, has a fragile ecosystem and is home to many rare plants.

LAND AND CLIMATE

Despite the small area of the state, the land is greatly varied. Rhode Island has two main land regions. The northwestern third of Rhode Island is part of the Eastern New England Upland, a hilly landscape with elevations as high as 800 feet above sea level. The rest of the state is part of the Coastal Lowlands. This area contains the coastline and a grouping of small islands known as the Narragansett Islands. Along the shore are sandy beaches and rocky cliffs. Narragansett Bay cuts deeply—about 28 miles—into the mainland.

The climate in Rhode Island is mild and humid. The average temperature is 29° Fahrenheit in January and 71°F in July. Rhode Island receives an average of 42 inches of precipitation every year. The weather is windy and, at times, unpredictable. Tropical storms in the summer and blizzards in the winter can sometimes switch to mild conditions in a matter of hours.

QUICK FACTS

At 812 feet above sea level, Jerimoth Hill is the highest point in Rhode Island.

The entire state is only 48 miles long from the northern tip to the most southern edge. It is only 37 miles long from east to west.

In 1938, the Great New England Hurricane brought winds of 91 miles per hour (mph) to Block Island. In Providence, winds reached 100 mph.

The South East Lighthouse on Block Island was built in 1875 to warn ships of the dangerous rocks and ledges along the coast.

The official state rock is cumberlandite, a rock with distinctive white markings.

NATURAL RESOURCES

Rhode Island may have few large mineral deposits, but the land has something else to offer—its soil. The soil in the western part of the state is rocky, while the soil in the eastern part near the ocean is sandy. The soil in the lowlands and on the islands is generally much better for cultivation. The richest soil is found near Narragansett Bay. Here, the soil is firm and not easily **eroded.** This makes it ideal for growing crops.

Numerous rivers have had a role in Rhode Island's economic success as well. The Blackstone, Pawtuxet, and Pawcatuck rivers provide fresh water and **hydroelectric** power to the people of Rhode Island.

QUICK FACTS

Potatoes are Rhode Island's most important field crop.

Although mining is not a large industry in the state, granite is the main mineral mined in Rhode Island. This mineral, which is found in the southwest, is used as a building material.

Rhode Island has been traditionally called "Little Rhody."

The Scituate Reservoir on the Pawtuxet River is the state's largest body of fresh water.

Other large bodies of water in Rhode Island include Watchaug Pond and Worden Pond.

Providence, Sakonnet, and Seekonk rivers are Rhode Island's main rivers. All three rivers are really arms of Narragansett Bay, making them saltwater rivers.

The soil around Narragansett Bay is very firm. It holds moisture for an entire growing season, making wine production a viable industry in the state.

PLANTS AND ANIMALS

Rhode Island is well forested, with more than 60 percent of the state covered in trees. Forests in the state consist of maples, oaks, ashes, birches, cedars, elms, and willows. Paper birches, which are also called canoe birches, thrive in the northernmost part of the state. The bark of these birches was peeled off in long strips and used by Native Americans to make birch-bark canoes. Rhode Island's "Christmas Greens" law protects trees and plants from being cut for Christmas holiday decorating. The law protects plants such as the American holly and sea lavender.

In the marshlands near Charlestown, asters and cattails bloom. Scarlet pimpernels can be found growing on the cliffs of Newport. These plants have small, individual flowers that are bell-shaped. Dogwoods, mountain laurels, rhododendrons, trilliums, and violets grow in the woodlands. Seaweed grows in Rhode Island's coastal waters. It anchors to the ocean floor with root-like ends. Unlike many plants, seaweed does not take in nutrients through its roots.

The state flower of Rhode Island is the violet. Rhode Island was the last state to adopt an official flower.

QUICK FACTS

Although it was once a whaling state, Rhode Island is trying to protect the northern right whale from extinction.

Four species of turtles and three species of whales are either endangered or threatened in Rhode Island.

The red maple is the state tree.

The black-eyed Susan, a wildflower that grows in Rhode Island, blooms in late summer.

Shorebirds and their habitat are protected by Rhode Island bird sanctuaries in order to preserve the population.

The animal population of Rhode Island is dominated by small mammals. Rabbits, gray squirrels, woodchucks, raccoons, minks, beavers, and although rare, foxes can also be found in the state's wilderness areas. White-tailed deer live on Prudence and Block Islands and are the largest wild mammals found in Rhode Island.

The state has a long shoreline along the Atlantic Ocean and there is a large variety of aquatic animals living in the waters. Cnidaria, a group of marine animals that have stinging **tentacles,** are common in the area. Cnidaria include jellyfish, corals, and sea anemones. Free-swimming jellyfish are saucer-shaped and are usually about the size of a human foot. Some types of jellyfish, however, can be as large as 6 feet in **diameter**!

Jellyfish are a common sight for beachgoers in Rhode Island. These marine animals should be treated with caution because their sting can cause rashes and muscle cramps.

QUICK FACTS

More than 300 species of birds have been identified in five wildlife refuges on the southern coast of Rhode Island.

The Block Island Conservancy is an organization of people interested in protecting the environment and natural beauty of Block Island.

Rhode Island has a state shell, the quahog. It was chosen on July 1, 1987. The shell of this clam was once used by local Native Americans as **currency.**

Newport is known for its colonial-era architecture.

QUICK FACTS

Hunter House, in Newport, was built in 1748 by the Deputy Governor of Rhode Island. It served as the headquarters of French naval commander Chevalier de Ternay during the American Revolution.

The only covered bridge on a public road in Rhode Island is located in Foster. Swamp Meadow Covered Bridge is a replica of bridges built in the area throughout the nineteenth century.

The oldest town building in the United States was built in 1796 in Foster, Rhode Island. It is still used for town meetings.

Rhode Island's early colonial history is evident in every major city. There are restored colonial homes in North and South Kingstown, a restored colonial inn in Coventry, and military museums and armories throughout the state.

TOURISM

Tourism is a vibrant industry in Rhode Island, and it supports more than 30,000 jobs. Annually, the state earns about $2 billion from tourism-related sales.

Visitors have much to see and do in the Ocean State. Rhode Island is steeped in history. For more than fifty years, **yachts** have competed just off the shore of Newport, in Narragansett Bay, for the famed America's Cup. This has earned the city of Newport the nickname, "Sailing Capital of the World." Tourists can learn about the history of America's Cup at the Herreshoff Marine Museum and at America's Cup Hall of Fame in Bristol.

Newport has enough attractions to keep a tourist busy for weeks, on topics ranging from local history to architecture. In the late 1700s and the early 1800s, some of the nation's wealthiest citizens lived in beautiful homes in Newport. Today, many of these homes are open to tourists. Belcourt Castle, which was once home to naval hero Oliver Hazard Perry, contains many antiques and treasures.

Belcourt Castle, originally a summer home for the wealthy Belmont family, is now a popular location for weddings and other special events.

The Rhode Island Red is a type of chicken that was first bred in the town of Compton. There is a monument dedicated to the breed in Adamsville.

QUICK FACTS

Early settlers in Rhode Island did not live on their own farms. They usually lived in nearby settlements and traveled to their farms each day.

Sheep farms are found in some of Rhode Island's inland areas.

The quonset hut, which was used as living quarters during World War II, was invented in Quonset, Rhode Island. The hut was made of metal and shaped like half a cylinder.

Farmland covers about 10 percent of the state. Rhode Island has about 700 farms.

Goods that are manufactured in Rhode Island are valued at about $5 billion.

INDUSTRY

In the Ocean State, large fishing operations and independent fishers alike haul in flounder, butterfish, and cod near Galilee, the location of a fish-processing plant. The annual fish catch in Rhode Island is valued at about $70 million. Lobster and quahogs, or hardshell clams, are the most valuable catches.

Agriculture, while less significant than it once was, remains important to Rhode Island's economy. Plant nurseries, turf harvesting, and the lumber industry are the chief agricultural activities. Greenhouse and nursery products account for about two-thirds of Rhode Island's agricultural income. These products include sod, ornamental trees, and shrubs. Dairy and poultry farms are also large contributors, as are potato farms and apple orchards.

The U.S. Navy is the largest employer in Rhode Island, after the state government. The Naval War College in Newport is one of the U.S. Navy's oldest institutions, having been in operation since 1884. Quonset Point Naval Air Station was a large base in Rhode Island during World War II, but the base was closed in 1974.

Point Judith is home to the port of Galilee, where each year more than 16 million pounds of fish and shellfish are unloaded.

GOODS AND SERVICES

The manufacture of goods was once the basis of Rhode Island's economy. In fact, following the American Revolution, the **textile** industry was Rhode Island's strongest economic activity. Samuel Slater, recognized as the founder of the United States textile industry, opened the nation's first spinning mill in Pawtucket. In recent years, however, the trade in goods such as textiles, jewelry, and electrical equipment has fallen behind the service sector. The service sector employs approximately 364,000 Rhode Islanders, accounting for nearly half of the personal income in the state. In contrast, the manufacturing sector constitutes about 11 percent of Rhode Islanders' total personal income.

The leading industries in the service sector include private health care, law firms, and computer programming companies. With New England's second-largest bank headquartered in Rhode Island, finance is also important to the state. Citizens Bank employs more than 8,200 people who work in any one of the bank's 330 branches.

Rhode Island has a strong tourism industry. The official travel ambassador of the state is the toy, Mr. Potato Head.

QUICK FACTS

G-Tech, the world's largest on-line lottery provider, has its main headquarters in Rhode Island.

Rhode Island businesses include American Power Conversion, a manufacturer of computer cable and power supply equipment; Brown & Sharpe, a manufacturer of navigation equipment; and KVH, a maker of medical supplies and equipment.

The now illegal practice of child labor in Rhode Island mills began with the first textile mill—the Slater Mill. By 1830, 55 percent of the workers at the mill were children. Many of them had to work long hours for less than $1 a week.

All of Rhode Island's electric power is produced by steam turbine plants.

Located on the Blackstone River in Pawtucket, Slater Mill is now a historic site and museum.

Rhode Island is the jewelry capital of the world. Twenty-five percent of the U.S. jewelry industry is concentrated in this state—the smallest state in the nation.

Some of Rhode Island's most important manufactured items are commonly found on necks and fingers and dangling from earlobes—jewelry! As early as 1794, the state had made a gleaming name for itself in this industry. Nehemiah Dodge from Providence came up with a method, called plating, to cover inexpensive metals with precious metals. This **innovation** helped Rhode Island become the nation's jewelry-making center.

Rhode Island is still highly respected for its accomplished silversmiths and jewelers. More than 35,000 people manufacture and distribute jewelry in the state. Prominent manufacturers operating in the state include Calibri, Sardelli, Monet, Danecraft, and Tiffany & Co. In 1999, Rhode Islanders were pleased to hear Tiffany's plans to build a jewelry manufacturing facility in Cumberland, creating about 450 jobs in the state. Tiffany & Co. is an internationally acclaimed jeweler, with stores throughout the world.

QUICK FACTS

The Gorham Manufacturing Company is a world leader in the silverware industry. Formed in 1831 by Jabez Gorham, the company made coins and silver-plate flatware. Today, the company continues the tradition as the manufacturer of many elegant flatware designs.

The first hand-operated cotton-spinning jenny in the United States was built in Providence in 1787.

Narragansett Bay is home to numerous boat-building and servicing operations.

Swarovski is a large manufacturer of crystal and rhinestones in Rhode Island.

In 1835, Rhode Island's first railroad began operation. It provided service between Providence and Boston. Today, the Providence and Worcester Railroad provides freight service in the state.

Silversmiths with Gorham Manufacturing work on pieces such as this trophy for the Indianapolis 500. Silverware items from Gorham are popular collectibles.

Metacom was the leader of the Pokanokets, a tribe of the Wampanoag. His death in 1676 ended the Native-American resistance in New England.

QUICK FACTS

Before European settlement, the Pequots drove the Niantics out of Connecticut and then fought a major territorial war with the Narragansett in 1632.

King Philip's War, fought in 1675 and 1676, was a conflict in which the Native Americans of the region attempted to push out the New England colonists. About 2,000 Native Americans lost their lives in the struggle. Although many colonists were also killed, the colonies were not destroyed.

After King Philip's War, the Narragansett, Wampanoag, and Pequot joined the Niantics to form a new Native-American community. They took the name Narragansett.

FIRST NATIONS

The area now known as Rhode Island was inhabited more than 8,000 years ago by Native Peoples. There were five separate groups: the Niantic, the Nipmuck, the Pequot, the Wampanoag, and the largest group, the Narragansett. All of them were Algonquin and spoke the Algonquian language. In Algonquin cultures, men fished and hunted, while women planted, harvested, and prepared food. Women were also responsible for moving, building, and maintaining the bark huts known as wigwams.

In the early 1600s, approximately 7,000 Narragansett lived in the largest portion of what was to become Rhode Island, ranging from Warwick to South Kingstown and Exeter. The Wampanoag were situated around the bay islands and the Providence and Warwick area. The Nipmuks, a relatively smaller group that joined the Narragansett, inhabited the northwest corner of Rhode Island. The Niantics lived in the Charlestown and Westerly areas.

Algonquian-speaking groups lived in fortified villages. Each lodge housed a large family.

Henry Hudson's obsessive quest for the Northwest Passage eventually led to the mutiny of his crew. Hudson was cast adrift, never to be seen again.

EXPLORERS AND MISSIONARIES

European exploration of Rhode Island began about 500 years ago. Portuguese sailor Miguel Corte-Real is thought to have traveled along the Rhode Island coast in 1511. In 1524, Giovanni Verrazano came upon the area while searching for the **Northwest Passage** on behalf of King Francis I of France. Verrazano explored Narragansett Bay and Block Island. Some historians believe that he may have described the island as being approximately the same size as the Island of Rhodes in the Mediterranean Sea. Later, explorers mistakenly thought that Verrazano had been describing the place known by Native Americans as "Aquidneck." Explorers renamed it Rhode Island.

In 1614, a Dutch explorer, Adriaen Block, visited Rhode Island while mapping the territory that Henry Hudson had explored earlier. Block was the first European to sail into Long Island Sound. He charted Long Island, showing it as a land mass separate from the Island of Manhattan. He also came across Block Island, and named it after himself.

The Verrazano-Narrows Bridge in New York City and the Verrazano Monument at New York's Battery Park are both named after Giovanni Verrazano.

In 1613, Dutch explorer Adriaen Block lost his ship in a fire and had to build a new one from trees that he and his crew chopped down on Manhattan Island. They named the new 44-foot ship *Restless*.

It is thought that Portuguese sailor Miguel Corte-Real carved his name and a number of symbols into Dighton Rock in Rhode Island's Taunton River.

When Giovanni Verrazano discovered Block Island, he described it as "an island in the form of a triangle, distant from the mainland ten leagues, about the bigness of the Island of Rhodes." He named Block Island "Luisa" after the Queen Mother of France.

In the seventeenth century, maps of Rhode Island were of great value to the area's early explorers and settlers.

EARLY SETTLERS

Roger Williams established the first working democracy in the Providence colony.

Providence Plantations was the first permanent settlement in Rhode Island. It was established by Roger Williams in 1636. Williams, an English member of the clergy, and others left the Massachusetts Bay colony to pursue their own religious beliefs. They purchased a large piece of land from two Narragansett chiefs, Canonicus and Miantonomo, on which to establish a settlement. Other groups seeking religious freedom soon followed. Anne and William Hutchinson, William Coddington, and John Clarke founded Portsmouth in 1638. There, they were free to practice their religion, Antinomianism, a sect similar to that of the Quakers. Not long after, various followers of this movement spread out to establish new settlements nearby.

In 1643, Samuel Gorton, John Greene, and others began a new settlement on Rhode Island. They left the Providence colony because it operated independently of English law. They felt that they could only find freedom while under the protection of the English. By the time the movement of Rhode Island's colonists began to slow down, there were four separate settlements in the state.

QUICK FACTS

William Blackstone, an Anglican clergy member, came to Rhode Island in the mid-1600s. He built a home by Lonsdale, near the banks of the river that came to be named after him.

Some of the earliest settlers seeking religious freedom in Rhode Island included Baptists (1639), Quakers (1657), Jews (1658), and Huguenots (1686).

The baby daughter of pilgrims John and Priscilla Alden is buried at Little Compton. She was the first child born to the New England colonists.

Roger Williams, the founder of Rhode Island, was born in London, England in 1602.

Settler's Rock at Sandy Point marks the landing spot of the first settlers to colonize Block Island.

The First Baptist Church was founded by Roger Williams in 1638. It still stands in Providence today.

Roger Williams pushed to unite the four Rhode Island settlements in order to protect themselves from neighboring colonies. In 1643, the English parliament granted a charter to Roger Williams that recognized the settlements as a colony. Later, in 1663, King Charles II granted a Royal Charter to Rhode Island and Providence Plantations, the official name of the state, promising religious freedom, self-government, and independence. This charter remained law until 1843. It was the most liberal charter granted by England during the colonial period, and many of its guarantees served as the foundation for the rights and freedoms established in the United States Constitution.

Due to the fertile soil and moderate temperatures, many Rhode Islanders were able to establish large farms and plantations. Still, African Americans were made to work as slaves on much of the land. Wealthy Newport merchants exported plantation products via large fleets of ships. Rhode Island's goods were sent to other English colonies in the United States and the West Indies.

Gray's Grist Mill, which has been stone grinding grains since 1675, is still in operation today.

POPULATION

Providence has a population of about 174,000, but it serves as a metropolitan center for close to 1 million people.

The population of Rhode Island is slightly more than 1 million people. About a sixth of Rhode Islanders live in Providence. The state is densely populated, with 1,003 people per square mile. Compared to the national average of 79 people per square mile, Rhode Islanders are quite "close" to their neighbors.

The earliest European settlers to Rhode Island were English Protestants of various denominations. Because of their religious tolerance, the state also attracted Irish, Huguenots, and Jews during the colonial period. Over the following centuries, waves of immigrants have added to Rhode Island's population. Irish Catholics settled in Providence, Pawtucket, and Newport in the 1820s, and French Canadians immigrated during the Civil War. Germans and Eastern Europeans arrived in the late 1800s.

Today, 85 percent of Rhode Islanders are of European descent, 8.7 percent are Hispanic American, 4.5 percent are African American, 2.3 percent are Asian American, and 0.5 percent are Native American. The remaining are Hawai'ian, Pacific Islander, or of another background.

Hispanic Americans make up the largest minority group in Rhode Island.

QUICK FACTS

About 14.5 percent of the population is 65 years of age or older. The national average is 12.4 percent.

The occurrence of child poverty in Rhode Island is lower than the national average. Child poverty in the state is estimated to be 17.3 percent. The national average is about 20 percent.

Nearly 60 percent of Rhode Islanders own their own home.

Newport shared the role of state capital with Providence from 1854 to 1900, when Providence became the sole state capital.

POLITICS AND GOVERNMENT

The first state constitution was the Royal Charter of 1663, which was granted by King Charles II. The most recent state constitution was adopted in 1986.

There are three branches of government: executive, legislative, and judicial. The governor serves as head of the executive branch of Rhode Island. He or she is elected to a 4-year term. The lieutenant governor, secretary of state, attorney general, and treasurer also serve 4-year terms. The governor has **veto** power and the authority to appoint department heads. The General Assembly has a legislature composed of 50 senators and 100 representatives. Rhode Island has a three-tier judiciary, with a Supreme Court serving as the last court of appeal after the superior courts and the district courts. Supreme Court judges are elected by the members of the General Assembly.

QUICK FACTS

The Declaration of Independence was signed at the Old State House in Providence.

Prior to 1854, Rhode Island had five state capitals operating at the same time: Providence, Newport, East Greenwich, Bristol, and South Kingstown. The General Assembly would travel from one capital to another on a rotating schedule. Providence became the sole capital in 1900.

Food and prescription drugs are exempt from Rhode Island's sales tax.

Providence, the state capital, is known as "The Renaissance City."

CULTURAL GROUPS

The Native-American Narragansett Tribe has a strong presence in Rhode Island. Although the Narragansett sold their communal lands to the state in 1880, they worked to preserve their cultural traditions and established a registry to keep track of members. In 1934, the Narragansett adopted an elective form of government to select their chief and council. In 1977, they recovered 1,800 acres of their land from the United States government.

The traditional culture of the Narragansett has been passed down from generation to generation and is still strong today. For instance, the **powwow** is a time to come together in dance and song. The Narragansett gather every August to celebrate the Annual Meeting Powwow and Green Corn Festival. Today, a majority of the 2,400 descendants of the original Narragansett that were registered in 1880 live in Washington and Providence counties. Smaller numbers are scattered throughout the rest of Rhode Island, as well as Connecticut and Massachusetts.

Rhode Island hosts many musical events, including the Cajun Bluegrass Festival, held every September at the Stepping Stone Ranch.

The Black Regiment of Rhode Island was one of the nation's first African-American regiments.

Although the percentage of African Americans living in Rhode Island today is considerably smaller than that of the national average, their early contribution to the state is significant. During the American Revolution, African Americans in New England, many of whom were slaves, supported the American colonies. While many states did not allow African Americans to take up the fight for independence, Rhode Island had one of the only regiments that was comprised mainly of African Americans. Known as the Black Regiment of Rhode Island, these soldiers played an important role in the Battle of Rhode Island by preventing the English from overtaking the Continental Army. After the American Revolution, some of the very same soldiers joined a new battle. Many became leaders in **abolition** movements throughout the North.

Today, the Rhode Island Black Heritage Society in Providence collects and preserves material of historical value relating to the role of African Americans in Rhode Island. Also, a monument dedicated to the Black Regiment of Rhode Island stands in Portsmouth.

Bristol has celebrated Independence Day since 1785—longer than any other community in the nation.

ARTS AND ENTERTAINMENT

For those interested in visual arts, Rhode Island has much to offer. The Newport International Film Festival, which was established in 1998, features independent and foreign films every June. A major highlight of this event is a outdoor film screening held at the International Tennis Hall of Fame in Newport.

The Rhode Island School of Design Museum has more than 85,000 works of art in its collection. Works include classical art from Greece, Rome, China, India, Egypt, and France, as well as masterpieces dating from the Middle Ages to the present. Pendleton House, a wing of the museum, was built in 1906 to display Charles L. Pendleton's remarkable collection of eighteenth- and nineteenth-century furniture and decorative arts. Pendleton House also exhibits the museum's large collection of American painting and sculpture, English ceramics, Chinese porcelain, and French wallpaper.

During Waterfire, in Providence, about 100 fires are lit along the banks of the Providence River.

For those who enjoy listening to music and watching dance performances, Rhode Island is the place to be. A variety of musical styles are represented in Rhode Island. The Rhode Island Philharmonic Orchestra, the Providence Singers, and the annual Rhode Island Chamber Music Concerts are some of the best examples of classical music companies in the state.

Those interested in ballet can take in the State Ballet of Rhode Island, Festival Ballet of Rhode Island, and Rhode Island's Ballet Theater. The State Ballet is Rhode Island's first professional company. The Festival brings guest and touring companies to Rhode Island audiences from October to June. Rhode Island's Ballet Theater prepares young dancers for professional classical companies.

A majority of the state's dance and theater companies are based in Providence. The Trinity Repertory Company, for example, is well known for its cutting edge performances. The dancers and choreographers at Groundwerx Dance Theater have been presenting traditional and modern dance performances since 1986.

The Rhode Island Philharmonic Orchestra has a music school that instructs 1,200 students on 35 different instruments.

The State Ballet of Rhode Island was founded in 1960.

QUICK FACTS

Galway Kinnell, born in Providence, is a well-known twentieth-century poet.

H. P. Lovecraft, one of the first writers of the modern horror novel, was born in Providence.

Author and actor Spalding Gray from Barrington is best known for his quirky **monologues.**

NewGate Theater hosts a festival of new works every winter entitled "Test Tube Theater."

George M. Cohan, a musician from the early twentieth century, is known for composing the songs, "I'm a Yankee Doodle Dandy" and "You're a Grand Old Flag." Cohan was born in Providence in 1878.

A tuna-fishing tournament is held yearly on Rhode Island and Block Island Sounds.

SPORTS

The East Bay Bike Path is a 14.5-mile pathway that extends from Providence to Bristol.

Narragansett Bay is one of the largest saltwater recreational areas in New England. With more than 2,300 acres of beautiful parks on six islands, many residents take part in a variety of outdoor activities. Biking and hiking are just a few of the activities enjoyed in Rhode Island. The state's small size makes the bicycle not only ideal for recreation and exercise, but also for transportation. Block Island is especially well-suited to cycling, with spectacular scenery and winding roads.

Hikers can explore the varied terrain of Rhode Island. The southern and eastern areas of the state are relatively flat, with gently rolling hills. The northern and western sections, however, rise abruptly through dense woodlands. Many hikers head to the numerous islands, where they may encounter plants and animals that are found in such coastal areas.

Rhode Island has more than 100 miles of sandy beaches. Visitors can enjoy a day at Crescent Beach, on Block Island, located south of the mainland.

Newport was the site of the America's Cup Yacht Race from 1920 until 1983. The competition that determined the fastest racing **schooner** has been waged since 1851, when Great Britain's Royal Yacht Club offered to race its schooners against a challenger from the United States. The American won the race, beating the entire Royal Yacht Club. A trophy was brought to the United States and named America's Cup. It was put on display at the New York Yacht Club. In 1983, an Australian challenger won the America's Cup. This was the first time a challenger beat a U.S. yacht in 132 years.

Rhode Island is widely known as "The Sailing Capital of the World. "

For tennis lovers, the oldest public grass courts in the United States can be found at the International Tennis Hall of Fame. This museum is located in the Newport Casino. The Hall of Fame brings professional tennis competition to Newport each year. The Tennis Hall of Fame Museum features displays, artifacts, and exhibits that cover more than a century of tennis history.

The International Tennis Hall of Fame preserves tennis history by staging old-fashioned tennis matches.

Brain Teasers

1

TRUE OR FALSE?

The oldest schoolhouse in the United States is in Rhode Island.

Answer: True. The schoolhouse was built in Portsmouth in 1716.

2

Roger Williams was the founder of which church?

Answer: Roger Williams founded the First Baptist Church.

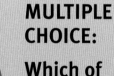

3

MULTIPLE CHOICE:

Which of the following individuals was born in Rhode Island?

a) Actor Harry Anderson

b) Sea captain Robert Gray

c) Inventor Stephen Wilcox

d) All of the above

Answer: d. All of the above.

4

Did Adriaen Block, the namesake of Block Island, discover the Northwest Passage?

Answer: No, Block never did find the mythical Northwest Passage.

5

What famous "summer cottage" is found in Newport?

Answer: Far more than a "summer cottage," The Breakers is a magnificent landmark in Newport. Designed in 1893, The Breakers was owned by the Vanderbilt family. The Vanderbilts established the family fortune in steamships, and later, in the New York Central Railroad.

6

What does the statue at the top of the State Capitol in Providence depict?

Answer: The statue depicts a figure known as "The Independent Man."

7

TRUE OR FALSE?
Brown University has always gone by this name.

Answer: False. Brown University was formerly called Rhode Island College. It was founded in 1764.

8

MULTIPLE CHOICE:

Redwood Library and Athenaeum is:

a) The oldest library building in the United States

b) The library containing the largest Rhode Island historical collection

c) Not a library at all

Answer: a. It is the oldest library in the United States.

FOR MORE INFORMATION

Books

Edwin S. Gaustad. *Liberty of Conscience: Roger Williams in America*. Valley Forge: Judson Press, 1999.

Paula M. Bodah. *Rhode Island: The Spirit of America*. New York: Harry N. Abrams, 2000.

Mary Lee Settle. *I, Roger Williams*. New York: W.W. Norton & Co., 2001.

Web Sites

You can also go online and have a look at the following Web sites:

50 States: Rhode Island
www.50states.com/rdisland.htm

Visit Rhode Island
www.visitrhodeisland.com

Rhode Island Government
www.state.ri.us

Some Web sites stay current longer than others. To find other Rhode Island Web sites, enter search terms such as "Providence," "New England," "Roger Williams," or any other topic you want to research.

GLOSSARY

abolition: the movement to put an end to slavery in the United States

coniferous: evergreen trees and shrubs, such as spruce and pine

currency: any form of money that is used as a means of exchange

diameter: a straight line that passes through the center of a circle and touches the circle at each end

eroded: to be worn away

hydroelectric: water-generated power

innovation: the creation of something new or different

monologues: dramatic or comic routines presented entirely by a single performer

Northwest Passage: a route through North America from the Atlantic Ocean to the Pacific Ocean

oceanographic: the branch of physical geography dealing with the ocean

powwow: a Native-American celebration

ratify: to support by expressing consent

schooner: a boat with a foremast and a mainmast

synagogue: a Jewish temple or house of worship

tentacles: limb-like features on certain animals, especially invertebrates (animals without a backbone), used for feeling, grasping, or locomotion

textile: woven products such as cloth, tapestries, rugs, or other fabrics

tolerated: to allow a certain practice or belief

veto: the power to cancel or postpone decisions within government

yachts: light, sailing vessels for racing

INDEX

American Revolution 6, 12, 14, 23
America's Cup 12, 27
Atlantic Ocean 4, 5, 11

Belcourt Castle 12
Black Regiment of Rhode Island 23
Block, Adriaen 17, 19, 28
Block Island 5, 6, 8, 11, 17, 18, 25, 26, 28
Bristol 12, 21, 23, 26

Coastal Lowlands 8

Eastern New England Upland 8

fishing 4, 7, 13, 16

Galilee 13
Gorham Manufacturing Company 15

International Tennis Hall of Fame 24, 27

Jerimoth Hill 5, 8
jewelry manufacturing 7, 14, 15

Little Compton 6, 18

Narragansett Bay 5, 7, 8, 9, 12, 15, 17, 26
Native Peoples (Native Americans) 10, 11, 16, 17, 20, 22
New England 4, 5, 6, 14, 16, 17, 18, 19, 23, 24, 26
Newport 5, 6, 10, 12, 13, 19, 20, 21, 22, 23, 24, 26, 27, 29
Newport International Film Festival 24

Perry, Oliver Hazard 12, 19
Providence 4, 5, 6, 7, 8, 15, 16, 18, 19, 20, 21, 23, 24, 25, 26, 27, 29

Rhode Island School of Design Museum 24

Slater, Samuel 14

Verrazano, Giovanni 17

Williams, Roger 6, 18, 19, 28